What You Should Know When Looking for a Job in Today's Marketplace

A STEP BY STEP APPROACH TO THE JOB SEARCH
A FIELD MANUAL FOR THE TIMES

Dr. Richard A. Wittmeyer, CMC

©Dr. Richard A. Wittmeyer – Strategic Performance Solutions, Inc. 2009

This publication is designed to provide accurate and authoritative information in regard to the subject matter and is sold with the understanding that the author is not engaged in rendering legal, accounting or other professional service. If legal advice or other expert assistance is required, the services of a competent professional person could be sought.

Printed in Victoria, BC, Canada.

Order this book online at www.trafford.com
or email orders@trafford.com
Most Trafford titles are also available at major online book retailers.

ISBN: 978-1-4269-2009-7

Library of Congress Control Number: 2009940189

Our mission is to efficiently provide the world's finest, most comprehensive book publishing service, enabling every author to experience success. To find out how to publish your book, your way, and have it available worldwide, visit us online at www.trafford.com

Trafford rev. 1/8/10

 www.trafford.com

North America & international
toll-free: 1 888 232 4444 (USA & Canada)
phone: 250 383 6864 ♦ fax: 812 355 4082

About the Author

Dr. Richard A. Wittmeyer, CMC, is a behavioral scientist and an accomplished entrepreneur and international business consultant with a notable record of success in human resources, talent acquisition, career and performance management and strategic organizational development.

Richard has over 30 years of experience as a nationally recognized public seminar leader, and has personally educated executives in the art of interviewing, talent acquisition and placement, leadership, motivation, pro-active employee relations strategy and talent management initiatives.

Dr. Wittmeyer's skill in communicating thought provoking concepts has frequently attracted national media recognition, including The Wall Street Journal, Success Magazine and PBS Television for his work in employee relations, talent acquisition and best in class organizational strategy. An astute change leader, Richard and his staff at Strategic Performance Solutions, Inc continue to provide tactical execution of management strategies that align with corporate goals.

Dedication

This book is dedicated to my wife Carol for it was with her help, encouragement and support that guided me through this undertaking. I wanted to develop an easy to understand self-help process that would assist people in their position search during periods of transition. Carol offered the inspiration and assistance to do so.

Dr. Richard A. Wittmeyer

Author's Acknowledgments

Whenever a publication is created it is generally done as a collaborative venture and I owe a great deal of gratitude to others in this effort:

Josh Nobiling, illustrator and sensational artist who sketched the appropriate illustrations for this book.

Rebekah Fowler, Ph.D. candidate and manuscript reviewer who took the time to ensure that the document made sense.

Jeff Phillips, Executive Recruiter with GRN who provided his expertise and technical assistance during the development of this project.

Dr. Louise Hickman, Ph.D. retired former Department Head of the Business Department at Morehead State University who provided expertise and technical advisement.

Preface

This book is for you if you have been laid off and are beginning a new chapter in your career, are anticipating a reduction in force at your company and feel your job is in jeopardy, are new to the job market and want to learn more about the hiring process or you feel it is time for a change and want to get a leg up in your job search.

Written in the form of a field manual that everyone can understand, the information in this book provides a complete process that will educate you in the skills required to land the position you want. It assists you in taking control of your employment future and in making those critical choices that are right for you.

Each chapter is loaded with practical information and concrete examples that you can use during your job search. From identifying your strengths, to constructing a resume that sells, to putting your best foot forward during the interview, you will develop the skills that will help put you ahead of your competition.

When you've landed that new position you can be satisfied in knowing that all of your planning, execution, and effort have paid off.

Dr. Richard A. Wittmeyer

A Reminder for Those in Transition

At the end of the day you are still a spouse, parent, grandparent, child, baseball coach, or soccer dad or mom to those people who care most about you. Keep active in your previous interests during this phase of your life or you will miss the many blessings of living.

Remember that a portion of what you are is wrapped up in your job. But, it isn't the total sum of who you are. Don't let this situation sap you of your energy and your personality. Keep everything in perspective.

If you are active in your place of worship, maintain that enthusiasm. Maintain your friendships; get out of the house and explore new interests. Take walks with your family. Look upon this time of transition as a bump in the road, not the end of the road. Be patient; expect the best, and remember that you are not alone in your job seeking efforts.

Testimonials

The information contained in this book assisted me while seeking a position with the U.S. Federal Marshals. I followed the examples in the construction of my resume and again during the interviewing process. It proved to be extremely worthwhile.

SJ
Patrol Officer
SLC Police Department

I have been developing a track record of career success for many years but felt that my last position was not taking me in the direction I wanted to travel. After using the job- seeking fundamentals presented in this book, I was successful in being offered the position I wanted.

The information is presented in a down to earth, real world manner that everyone can understand. All I needed to do was to follow the steps. It certainly worked for me. Today I am in a position I enjoy with colleagues I respect.

MW
Accounting
GB Electric Co.

In this book Rich has been able to break down the fundamentals of how to prepare a resume, research for opportunities, find and contact prospective employers, prepare for an interview, and how to interview with the hiring manager into a series of well constructed building blocks. Along the way candidates test themselves in a series of self-assessments designed to better improve the candidates understanding of where they have been and how to get to where they want to go. When job seekers follow Rich's process, they will undoubtedly be the best prepared candidates applying for the position.

JP
Executive Recruiter
Global Recruiters Network (GRN)

What You Should Know When Looking for a Job in Today's Marketplace

TOPICS

WORKSHEETS AND EXAMPLES

CHAPTER 1: INTRODUCTION

You have come to a place in your career where you are beginning a new adventure. Perhaps you are anticipating a reduction in the work force and think your job is in jeopardy, or you feel it is time for a change and want to get a leg up in your job search. Maybe you've suffered a lay off or a reduction in the work force and feel that this job loss is a real step backwards for your career. In all three of these cases, people are uncertain what to do next or even how to go about pursuing a new position in today's tight job marketplace.

Seeking a New Job Opportunity

No matter the reason for leaving your last position it is unfair to assume that all you need to do is sit and wait for that new opportunity to come your way. It takes work on your part to land that next position. So let's get started!

What you do now is critical to your career success. Don't let the situation control you. You take control of the situation. Don't be a victim of circumstances. Develop a vision for success. Start to learn the job search methods presented in this book and develop a plan of action.

The Hiring Process: Yesterday versus Today

Years ago it was fairly easy to find a new position. Search firms would call you with a position opening and you could take your time selecting between job offerings. Or, friends contacted you with tips that a company down the road was hiring and needed people with your skills. All that you needed to do was to update your resume from time to time and everything fell into place.

Today we have a different situation. The marketplace is crawling with competition for those jobs. It is not realistic to sit back and think that a company will find you. You need to put together a well-thought-out action plan to seek the job you want.

This book will assist you in setting new goals and evaluating new career options. It will help you manage your job transition and employment campaign in a realistic, systematic, and organized way.

Information Gathering

By definition, a job transition is a well executed and strategic move from one job opportunity to another. To begin your search efforts, look at this transition as a time to explore and evaluate many different career opportunities. You may wish to start with the industry with which you are most familiar, but consider branching out into other industries that are of interest to you. Your former employer, for example, might have been in the mining industry. After a thorough job search, however, you find that the mining industry is reducing its workforce while alternative energy sources may be seeking a person with your work history, talents and skills.

There are those people who, after a job loss, have purposely chosen not to get back into their former industry. They have seen their job loss as a relief, among other things, because they felt trapped and had no way of leaving because of the income it provided.

Now that you have the opportunity, take a step back for a moment and assess what you want to be doing a few years from now. You may begin to realize that it's time for a industry change. Remember to keep your job options open.

Self Discovery

As you continue to explore various industries and options, you might also ask the following questions: **"Why would a company want me? What do I have to offer? What do I bring to the table?"** Let's compile the answers to these questions.

<u>What the Recruiters Want:</u>

Recruiters and company hiring officers alike are in the business of seeking the best candidates for the open position. They do this by electronically sorting through the many resumes they receive in an attempt to match the candidate's qualifications and qualities to the position requirements. Qualities should include:

- job accomplishments
- skill sets
- strengths
- work experiences
- training and education

The closer the match, the greater the opportunity the candidate will have in landing that interview.

Four Areas of Exploration

What You Have to Offer:

The better you are in identifying and presenting the work experience and qualities that you bring to the table, the better prepared you will be in designing a resume that will sell. To begin the process of self discovery, we will focus our attention in four areas that provide the greatest amount of information about you. They include:

- Job Accomplishments. These are noteworthy achievements that you contributed to your job that were recognized by others as a special act. These acts influenced your employers' bottom line or added value to the business.
- Job Skills. These are technical competencies that you were professionally trained and educated in, such as sales, cost accounting, human resources, specific apprentice programs, and on the job certifications that you hold.
- Personal Attributes. These are personal qualities and assets. Those non-technical characteristics, skills, and strengths that you have taken upon yourself to learn and practice on the job. You used these personally developed aptitudes to accomplish your work successfully. These skills and strengths are universal in that they may be transferred to any job that you seek. They may be described by words and phrases like:
  o detail oriented
  o problem solver
  o thorough
  o polished
  o tactful
  o communicator
  o thoughtful
- Special Acknowledgements and Noted Distinctions. These are special accomplishments that go beyond job achievements. These include books, instructional manuals and other publications you've written, patents you hold, honors you have achieved, and lecturing engagements and seminar presentations you have made. Military honors and security clearances are also included in this section.

Putting Your Information Together

Let's now identify and construct your own list of accomplishments, technical job skills, personal attributes, and special acknowledgements by completing the following exercise.

In order to develop your information for the four areas of exploration, an example worksheet has been designed to assist you. This worksheet found on page 8, is divided into four distinct sections for easy identification.

Section 1 of the worksheet is designed to highlight your **job accomplishments.** Since we are collecting information from throughout your career, it is important that you list the specific job accomplishment, the name of the company, and the position you were holding at the time the accomplishment was achieved. List as many accomplishments as you can on the worksheet.

Key words that identify **accomplishments** include:

- Designed
- Developed
- Reduced
- Generated
- Led
- Saved
- Increased
- Improved
- Implemented
- Advised
- Achieved
- Directed
- Established
- Created
- Authored
- Launched

Some examples of selected accomplishments include:

- <u>Designed</u> a training program that aligned with corporate reforms to instruct new employees in workplace culture (XYZ Company, as Training Manager)
- <u>Reduced</u> operating costs by 12% of budgeted expenses (ABC Company, as Supervisor).
- <u>Led</u> a broad range of team activities that <u>eliminated</u> 7% waste (JKL Company, as Lead Person).
- <u>Initiated</u> cost control measures that <u>increased</u> significant cash flow by $2M annually (MNO Company, as CFO).

Next, list your **job skills, technical experience, and certifications** by filling in Section 2 of the worksheet. Remember that job skills are technical skills that you learned either through formal job training programs, through formal education, or through on-the-job training and apprentice programs. Examples of technical skills include:

- Teaching
- Real Estate
- Law
- Data Processing
- Roof Bolting
- Truck Driving
- CDL
- Heavy Equipment Operator
- Law Enforcement
- Human Resources
- Masonry
- Carpentry

Section 3 is designed for you to list your **personal attributes**. Remember that this section is a collection of what you enjoy doing, are good at doing, or have a talent for doing, and may include:

- Communicator
- Writer
- Trouble Shooter
- Problem Solver
- Team Builder
- Motivator
- Mentor
- Manager

Section 4 is designed for you to list your **special acknowledgments and notable distinctions.** Always remember to date your acknowledgements and distinctions when listing them. Examples may include:

- Silver Beaver Award - Boy Scouts of America Award - 2002
- Who's Who in America - 2003
- Books and Publications – The Assertive Manager – AMA Publications - 1999

On page 7 you will find an example of a completed worksheet for your review. After you review the example, go to the blank worksheet on page 8 to construct your own answers to the four sections. Attempt to develop at least six to eight statements for each section.

EXAMPLE   **WORKSHEET 1-1**
INFORMATION GATHERING

LIST EACH ACCOMPLISHMENT, THE COMPANY YOU WORKED FOR, AND THE JOB YOU WERE HOLDING

SECTION 1   AT THE TIME OF THE ACCOMPLISHMENT

- Designed training program that aligned with corporate reform to instruct new employees in workplace culture (ABC Company as Training Manger)
- Reduced operating costs by 12% of budgeted expenses (XYZ Company as Supervisor)
- Led broad range of team activities in operations that eliminated waste by 7% (JKL Company as Lead Person)
- Initiated cost control that maintained significant cash flow by 10% (MNO Company as CFO)
-
-

SECTION 2   JOB SKILLS AND TECHNICAL EXPERIENCE

- Training/Teaching
- Real Estate License
- Data Processing Skills Word, Excel, Power Point
- Machinery/Equipment/Equipment Operator, D2 Dozer
- Human Resources: Employment Law, Employee Relations, Program Development, Wage and Salary Administration
-

SECTION 3   PERSONAL ATTRIBUTES

- Communicator
- Trouble Shooter
- Writer
- Manager
- Problem Solver
-
-

SECTION 4   SPECIAL ACKNOWLEDGEMENT AND NOTABLE ACHIEVEMENTS

- Silver Beaver Award - Boy Scouts of America_2002
- Who's Who in America 2003
- Books/Publications – The Assertive Manager – AMA Publications 1999
-
-
-
-
-

EXAMPLE   **WORKSHEET 1-1**

INFORMATION GATHERING

LIST EACH ACCOMPLISHMENT, THE COMPANY YOU WORKED FOR, AND THE JOB YOU WERE HOLDING AT THE TIME

SECTION 1   OF THE ACCOMPLISHMENT

- _____
- _____
- _____
- _____
- _____
- _____

SECTION 2   JOB SKILLS AND TECHNICAL EXPERIENCES

- _____
- _____
- _____
- _____
- _____
- _____
- _____

SECTION 3   PERSONAL ATTRIBUTES

- _____
- _____
- _____
- _____
- _____
- _____
- _____

SECTION 4   SPECIAL ACKNOWLEDGEMENT AND NOTABLE ACHIEVEMENTS

- _____
- _____
- _____
- _____
- _____
- _____
- _____

COMPLETING WORKSHEET 1-2

Now that you have completed Worksheet 1-1 on page 8, select 5 of your strongest **Technical Skills** from your technical list found in Section 2 and place them below.

<u>Job Skills and Technical Experience</u>

- _____
- _____
- _____
- _____
- _____

Again, select what you consider to be 5 of your strongest **Personal Attributes** from your list in Section 3, Worksheet 1-1 and place them below.

<u>Personal Attributes</u>

- _____
- _____
- _____
- _____
- _____

Your Personal Attributes in Greater Depth:

Completing Worksheet 1-3

As you continue to develop the information to use for your resume, review Worksheet 1-2 above where you listed your 5 strongest **Personal Attributes**. Take each of the 5 Personal Attributes separately and provide examples of how you used the skill and when in your work history it was used. The section below will provide you with examples. Upon reviewing the examples, complete Worksheet 1-3 found on page 11.

Examples of Specific Attributes

<u>Attribute</u>**:** Communicator
   How you used it:
- Held daily morning production meetings with my team (XYZ Company as Line Supervisor).
- Communicated daily work plans and job assignments with precision and accuracy (XYZ Company and ABC Company as Production Coordinator).

<u>Attribute</u>: Writer

How you used it:

- Documented with accuracy written papers and production reports for the engineering team (QAZ Company as Administrative Coordinator).

<u>Attribute</u>: Managing Others

How you used it:

- Provided guidance and training to new employees during orientation programs (ABC Company as Lead Person).
- Had seven direct reports on crew requiring daily oversight (ABC Company as Supervisor).

NOTE: Move to Worksheet 1-3 on the next page and complete the exercise. Note as many attributes as you can.

PERSONAL ATTRIBUTES

WORKSHEET 1-3

List your personal attributes and how you used them in your work experience:

Attribute 1: _____

How you used it in your former job(s):

- _____
- _____
- _____
- _____

Attribute 2: _____

How you used it in your former job(s):

- _____
- _____
- _____
- _____

Attribute 3: _____

How you used it in your former job(s)

- _____
- _____
- _____
- _____

Attribute 4:_____

How you used it in your former job(s):

- _____
- _____
- _____
- _____

Attribute 5: _____

How you used it in your former job(s):

- _____
- _____
- _____

Targeting Your Job Search

The last portion of this information gathering chapter is designed to help you make personal decisions about your job future. The key to a targeted job search is to identify the job you want, in the industry in which you wish to be employed, and that will provide you with the ability to use your key talents and skills while fulfilling other personal needs. First, you must ask the question, "What am I seeking from my next position?" To help you answer this question we have two exercises for you to complete. The first exercise is an evaluation of six personal needs that are important to all job seekers to one degree or another. Known by the acronym CLAMPS, each letter of the acronym represents a specific job need. The second exercise is a paragraph that you will construct to sum up your total job requirements.

Let's take a look to see how this exercise applies to you.

The CLAMPS Assessment

To assist you in making an informed evaluation of your job needs, we have defined each specific need that you will be assessing.

These needs include:

Challenge - A job that will test your skills and abilities.

Location –A job that offers a suitable region/area of the country in which to reside.

Advancement – A job that will offer rapid opportunity for promotion and vertical mobility.

Money – A job that would offer better than average compensation for the requirements of the position.

People – A job that would require a great deal of interaction with others.

Security – A job that provides a safe workplace environment free from anxiety and stress.

The CLAMPS Needs Assessment Chart

WORKSHEET 1-4

This worksheet found on page 13 is a forced choice assessment. You will notice that there are six needs categories listed in the first column. Rank the 6 needs in the score column with 1 representing your most important need through 6, representing your least important need. Give each need only one ranking. You will use the top two selected needs when you complete Worksheet 1-5 found on page 14.

Clamps Worksheet 1-4 (continued)

CATEGORY	SCORE
Challenge	
Location	
Advancement	
Money	
People	
Security	

Now We'll Look at Your Job Requirements

Now that you have completed the CLAMPS Worksheet 1-4 above, we will move to Worksheet 1-5. Continue to think about your job future and complete the paragraph on the next page. An example of a completed paragraph is found below.

EXAMPLE 1-5

Meeting My Job Requirements

I am seeking the position of <u>Director of Human Resources</u> in the <u>manufacturing industry</u>, for a (underline one) large, <u>mid-sized</u>, small organization. This company will afford me the opportunity to use the following technical skills: <u>my human resources generalist skills in talent acquisition, benefits and compensation, project management, team building, strategic planning</u>, and the following personal attributes: <u>problem solving, trouble shooting and the ability to manage others</u>. It is important that the job I seek satisfies the two needs that are at the top of my CLAMPS ASSESSMENT LIST: the need for <u>people</u> and the need for <u>challenge.</u>

Now complete your own paragraph by filling in the blanks on the form on the next page.

13

Meeting My Job Requirements

WORKSHEET 1-5

I am seeking the position of _____ in the _____
                          (job title)   (type of industry)
industry, for a large, mid-sized, small organization. This company will afford me
              (underline one)
the opportunity to use the following technical skills: _____

_____, and the following personal attributes : _____

_____. It is important that the job I seek satisfies the

two needs that are at the top of my CLAMPS ASSESSMENT LIST:

the need for _____ and the need for _____.

NOTE: You have now completed the information gathering section. We will use this
information to construct your resume.

CHAPTER 2: THE RESUME

Awell constructed resume provides key information about you, your talents, skills, competencies, employment history, contributions, and achievements. See this resume as your sales brochure with you as the product.

As discussed in Chapter 1, recruiters and company hiring officers seek candidates whose knowledge, skills, abilities, and achievements match the position criteria. To accomplish their mission, high tech computer screening is used to flag information on a resume to determine candidate qualifications. Further, recruiters look at the completeness of the resume, seek gaps between employment dates, explore the frequency of job changes, and evaluate relevant experiences and previous positions that are compatible with the position being filled.

For these reasons you must focus carefully on the content of the resume. As you begin constructing this document, remember that a better resume gets you a better opportunity to be interviewed. The resume needs to convey a compelling reason for hiring you over other qualified candidates. Remember that the resume isn't about you, it's about what you can do for the hiring company. A well crafted resume addresses your potential, sparks interest, and entices others to want to find out more about you. With a well crafted resume combined with proper networking, web searching, postal campaigns, recruiter contacts, and by attending professional organization meetings where you are surrounded by people of like interest, you will get your campaign off to a solid start.

The Importance of the Resume

Constructing the resume is of utmost importance because it puts forward to the reader your strengths and accomplishments. The resume should be constructed in such a manner that it "sells" your brand. It should emphasize to the hiring organization your ability to add value and provide skills they are seeking.

For years people have developed the mentality of telling their story in the resume by describing what they did in the jobs they had. It was more of a history lesson than a resume revealing candidate potential. Imagine a visit to your friend's home; when you get there you find that you are expected to watch films of his summer vacation all evening. It would be enjoyable to him, but dull for you. Dull resumes generally never make the first interview. Be sure to build your resume in a manner that will captivate the reader.

Putting life in the resume means that you use **numbers and percentages to quantify your previous experience and positions.** The reader not only wants to know what you did on the job, but also how well you did it.

What Hiring Officers Are Looking for in the Resume

As hiring officers review candidate resumes, they have a series of standards that they abide by. These standards are summarized below.

<u>Hiring Officers</u>:
- Want to ensure that talented and competent people are hired for the open position.
- Don't want surprises when it comes to people and their qualifications. All information on the resume must be accurate and truthful.
- Want a candidate to be as good as other people already in the company they represent.
- Are interested in reducing training time by selecting the most qualified candidate.
- Want people with experience who are passionate about what they do.
- Want people who will be satisfied in their jobs and are not just looking for a career step to the next job opportunity.
- Want people who will be part of the team, not a "show boat" doing their own thing.
- Want people who possess similar qualities, values, and integrity as reflected in the company culture.
- Want people who show ingenuity and will contribute solutions to problems that are regularly faced.
- Want people who can quantify their accomplishments.

For these reasons the resume must be focused on your ability to contribute real numbers to the company goals. Demonstrate what you've saved or the value you've added to the bottom line of past employers. If your resume doesn't reflect what you can do for the hiring organization, you'll not get a second look.

Constructing Your Resume

There are three general resume formats that are used today. The format is the process of organizing your information. The organization of information depends upon what you want to emphasize in the document. Possible examples to be emphasized include: upward mobility, experience, achievements, quality of the organizations for which you've worked, and/or accomplishments that you've made. The three most common resume formats are listed on the next page in order of usage.

Reverse Chronological Resume

The Reverse Chronological Resume is designed around your work history. It begins with a high powered opening summary paragraph showcasing your marketable skills and achievements followed by a listing of your core competencies. Your employment history follows in chronological order with most recent employment listed first. Finally, your education and certifications/licenses you hold would be listed at the end of the document.

Functional Resume

The Functional Resume is designed around your strengths, abilities and accomplishments. It initially ignores chronological order of employment and focuses upon targeted results and achievements. This format also begins with a high powered opening summary paragraph about your marketable skills and core competencies in a manner similar to the Chronological Resume, but that's where the similarity ends.

The resume construction, instead, begins to focus directly upon your career accomplishments. This approach presents to the hiring officer a collection of your many talents and showcases the reasons for selecting you as a candidate. A very brief employment history would then follow that includes your previous employers, job titles, and dates of employment--nothing more. The last section of this format concludes with formal education, professional training, and any certifications you may hold. This format is the second most used resume format.

Hybrid Format

The Hybrid Resume is a combination of the Chronological and Functional formats. Realize that ONE SIZE DOES NOT FIT ALL in resume writing; a tailored resume to meet a targeted organization or position is most useful. The Hybrid fits this need.

Resume Construction in More Detail

The following provides you with a more in-depth, step-by-step explanation in the construction of both the Reverse Chronological and Functional Resume. You will find examples of each of these resumes after their individual step-by-step explanations.

A Step By Step Preparation of the Reverse Chronological Resume

Step 1: The resume header should always consist of the basic contact information and how you can be reached followed by the job title of the position you are seeking: Human Resources Executive, Business Analyst, Restaurant Server, etc.

Step 2: Provide a career profile paragraph including qualifications, personal attributes, targeted strengths, characteristics, etc. (anything that would identify you as the right choice for the position you seek), followed by no more than 6 selected achievements and qualifications. As a matter of form, bullets are used before each selected achievement.

<u>Step 3:</u> List specific core competencies and areas of expertise that are relevant to the position you seek. As a matter of form, bullets are again used before each specific competency. You may pull this information from the Section 2 and 3 of Worksheet 1-1, Chapter 1.

<u>Step 4:</u> A summary of your work history is next, listing the most recent employer first, followed by other employers listed in descending order, most recent to least recent, according to dates of employment. Provide the name, location, job title and a one or two line narrative about the company. Follow this by noting several accomplishments that you achieved in the position you previously held with that company. You may pull this information from Section 1 of Worksheet 1-1, Chapter 1.

Hiring officers are interested in the most recent ten to fifteen years of your career. Should you have a lengthy career, you may wish to use a section in your resume entitled **additional prior experience** where you would list any previous work history to include the company you worked for and position titles you held. Your dates of employment are optional. It is also your choice whether you wish to list any special achievements or not.

<u>Step 5:</u> List any formal education you have and certifications you hold. This information should begin with your most recent educational experience and move backward chronologically. You may pull this information from section 2 of Worksheet 1-1, Chapter 1.

If you are a college graduate, there is no need to list your high school in the educational section. If you have not completed college, list the high school from which you graduated followed by any college course work you've completed.

<u>Step 6:</u> Identify any acknowledgements, special achievements and notable distinctions such as licenses and patents you hold, books you have written, or papers you have presented. You may pull this information from Section 4 of Worksheet 1-1, Chapter 1.

<u>Step 7:</u> Identify any professional associations and business related memberships you hold. Include positions of leadership and dates.

An example of a reverse chronological resume appears on the following page.

Example 2-1

JOHN P. JONES

2703 Linden Court • Morris, IL 62959 • (h) 618-784-1111 • j.jones@mchsi.com

VP / DIRECTOR of HR

Comprehensive HR Leadership♦ Organizational Development ♦ Increased Profitability

Proactive, accomplished HR strategist with history of driving corporate-wide programs and initiatives that directly aligns with overall strategy and vision. Expertise in talent acquisition / training and leading organizational cultural change to enhance productivity, reduce costs, and streamline daily operations. Demonstrated strength at delivering large, complex projects for Fortune 500 and 1000 companies on time and within budget. Proficient at managing staff / labor relations to significantly improve employee satisfaction levels and reduce attrition while avoiding unionization. Adept at introducing performance management initiatives and establishing metrics and benchmarking systems. Polished professional with exceptional communication talents; frequent guest speaker / lecturer on HR, compliance, pro-active employee relations, talent management, total rewards, and diversity programs. Dedicated to aligning organizations with marketplace and human capital with company objectives to achieve both short-and long-term profit goals.

Selected Achievements

➢ Saved $11M in operations costs by initiating key process improvement strategies.

➢ Developed and structured team initiatives and change management strategies that reduced internal operating cost by up to 17% for client companies spanning diverse industries.

➢ Successfully led all aspects of HR for Robert's Tires the largest manufacturing facility for original equipment tires.

➢ Former President of Center for Creative Management, a D&B-listed HR/OD consulting firm with a staff of 22 and offices in Missouri, Florida, and Ohio.

➢ Drove initiative to reduce worker compensation claims, which saved $500K in first year with added $115K savings in first quarter of 2008.

➢ Reduced clients' organizational costs by 18% average via HR / change management strategies during M&A integrations.

Areas of Expertise

• Strategic Planning	• Multi-Site Operations	• Benefits / Compensation
• Recruiting / Staffing / Retention	• Employee / Labor Relations /CB/ Gvt Regs	• Project Management
• Talent Development / Training	• Union Free Status &De-certification	• Succession Planning
• Performance Management	• Policy / Procedure Development	• Total Rewards
• Change / Turnaround Leadership	• Financial / Budget Management	• Program Dev. / Delivery
• Start-up/Acquisitions	• Coaching / Mentoring	• Process Improvement

PROFESSIONAL SUMMARY

WHITE RIDGE ENERGY   Oak Brook, IL

Nation's largest independently owned and operated coal producer, with 15 mining facilities in eight states and 60 subsidiary companies that produce 30 million tons of coal / year; gross revenues of 2.6B

Director of HR   2004 to Present

➢ Drove all aspects of HR for Operations spanning 1,500 employees, four mines, one preparation plant and 15 of 60 subsidiary companies; provided leadership to ten direct / 34 indirect reports.

➢ Led special projects that directly contributed to 6% Company growth.

➢ Overhauled HR to create a state-of-the-art, best-in-class operation that aligned seamlessly with business plan and strategy.

➢ Played strategic role on senior leadership team that effectively directed Organization through several business challenges.

➢ Drove initiative to reduce worker compensation claims, which saved $500K in first year with added $115K savings in 2008.

➢ Initiated team strategy that increased productivity by 7%+ within three months and reduced mine costs by `$1.5M / month.

➢ Reduced turnover by 23% within six months by designing new intake programs, improving hiring practices, revamping training / orientation programs, and establishing clear employee goals, standards, and expectations.

➢ Authored and implemented policies and procedures that improved consistency of gement practices reducing employee complaints by 47%.

JOHN P. JONES

JENKINS COPPER, LTD

Nation's second-largest copper producer, revenues of $2.4B

Corporate Director – Organizational Effectiveness, HR Initiatives, and Organizational / Talent Development 1998 to 2004

➢ Created/delivered integrated strategic HR, organizational, and staff development initiatives and solutions Corporate-wide.

➢ Implemented change management / cultural reform to create a team-based, strategically aligned organization.

➢ Drove HR transition of several acquisitions from vertical business units to functional organizational structures.

➢ Improved corporate business performance by 7% by leading in-company HR / OD initiatives.

➢ Saved $11M in operations costs by initiating mining process improvement strategies.

➢ Reduced process controls 8% / increased Company efficiency 12% by developing staff of process improvement specialists.

➢ Added 14% productivity increase by directing program to achieve budgeted personnel status for field locations.

➢ Directly contributed to reorganization of Operation's business units, which increased stock value by 27%.

Experience up to 1998 includes President of Center for Creative Management, a D&B-listed HR / OD consulting firm with staff of 22 and offices in Missouri, Florida, and Ohio; provided HR solutions for a diverse client-listing nationwide.

➢ Reduced clients' organizational costs by 18% average via HR / change management strategies during M&A integrations.

➢ Led turnaround of Fortune 1000 firm with 1050 employees; achieved multi-million-dollar cash flow growth by developing HR teaming initiatives that increasing productivity 15% and product quality 20%.

➢ Drove strategy to achieve ISO-9002 registration for three chemical manufacturing / processing clients within 14 months.

➢ Saved average 18% in productivity costs / year for clients by facilitating positive union / management relationships.

➢ Designed and led client HR reorganization and administration initiatives to secure annual savings of $2.2M.

EDUCATION, CERTIFICATIONS & PROFESSIONAL DEVELOPMENT

Medford University, Albuquerque ◆ New Mexico
Master of Business Administration (MBA) ◆ Human Resources Management
Wood University ◆ Northfield, Vermont
Bachelor of Arts (BA) ◆ Psychology, and Business Administration
CMC (Certified Management Consultant) Certification ◆ The Institute of Management Consultants
Granted in human resources, organizational development, and process improvement practices
Professional Development: Six Sigma, AMA Assessment Center, and Harvard University Executive Leadership
US Military / Officers Branch and Tactics School ◆ Fort Benning, Georgia

---

ACHIEVEMENTS AND NOTABLE DISTINCTIONS

Penn State White Paper Presenter, Process Improvement, St. Louis, MO 2006
Author, The Supervisor as a Conference Leader, Genco 1987
Assert Yourself, AMR, International, 1998
National Congressional Committee Business Advisory Council, Illinois and Missouri, 2001 to 2006

PROFESSIONAL AFFILIATIONS & ASSOCIATIONS

President's Senatorial Inner Circle, Washington, D.C. ◆ Member, 1998 to 2005
AAIM, St. Louis Chapter, Human Resources/Organizational Development Executives ◆ Member, 2003 to present
Penn State/Colorado School of Mines, BPI Symposium - Denver, CO ◆ Co-chair, 2004 to 2007
Penn State Committee on Business Process Improvement in the Extractive Industries ◆ Member, 2004 to present
LMPCP Certified / UMWA-BCOA Consultant in Union / Management Relations ◆ 1999 to 2002

A Step By Step Preparation of the Functional Resume

NOTE: You will find two examples of the Functional Resume after this step-by-step explanation.

<u>Step 1:</u> Begin with the basic information about yourself and how you may be contacted, followed by the job title of the position you are seeking: Human Resource Manager, Restaurant Supervisor, Administrative Assistant, etc.

<u>Step 2:</u> Provide a career profile paragraph including qualifications, personal attributes, targeted strengths, characteristics, etc. (anything that would identify you as the right choice for the position you seek).

<u>Step 3:</u> List specific core competencies and areas of expertise you possess that are relevant to the position you seek. As a matter of form, bullets may be used before each specific competency you list. You may pull this information from Sections 2 and 3 of Worksheet 1-1, Chapter 1.

<u>Step 4:</u> You will now list a series of selected achievements from the past 10 to15 years of your work history that reflects upon your ability. At this step you are emphasizing targeted results.

<u>Step 5:</u> List your professional work experience with the name of the company, location, job title, and your dates of employment--nothing more. This step should list most recent employer first with others following in descending order.

<u>Step 6:</u> List any formal education, training, and certifications you hold.

<u>Step 7:</u> Identify any acknowledgements, special achievements, and notable distinctions. You may pull this information from Section 4 of Worksheet 1-1, Chapter 1.

<u>Step 8:</u> Identify any professional association memberships you hold. Include positions of leadership, if applicable, and dates.

The following two Functional Resume examples have been provided for easy reference. You will notice that in the first example we are emphasizing three areas of job achievement: Human Resources, Organization Development, and Consulting. In the second example we emphasize all achievements and results throughout a person's career.

Example 2-2

JOHN P. JONES

2703 Linden Court * Morris, IL 62959* (h) 618-784-1111 * j. jones@mchsi.com

VP/DIRECTOR OF HR
COMPREHENSIVE HR /OROGANIZATIONAL DEVELOPMENT

EXECUTIVE PROFILE

Results-focused entrepreneurial executive and consultant with a notable record of success in Human Resources, Strategic Organization Development, and Performance Management. Astute change leader able to provide alignment and tactical execution of HR management programs that aid corporate vision. Strong background in developing strategic business plans, improving and implementing processes, and developing workplace cultures. Persuasive consensus builder adept in cross-functional negotiation to achieve "win-win" outcomes. Published author and media contributor.

Core Competencies:

• Organizational Effectiveness	• Fortune 500 Leadership Consulting	• Regulatory Compliance
• Reducing Margin Costs	• Executive Management Placement	• Conflict Management
• Training & Development	• Talent Management	• ISO 9000 Certification
• Increasing productivity	• Employee/Labor Relations	• Succession Planning

SELECTED ACHIEVEMENTS

Human Resources
- Championed companywide program to achieve budgeted "manning" status for field locations resulting in additional man hour productivity increase of 14%.
- Introduced performance management programs that disaggregated individual performance appraisals from professional development and established metrics that aligned both individual and functional goals with business objectives.
- Realized an average 18% savings in annual productivity costs for key clients by leading executive decision makers in successfully creating a proactive union/management workplace relationship by way of LMPCP.

Organizational Development
- Led turnaround of Fortune 1000 firm with 550 personnel; achieved multi-million-dollar cash flow growth by increasing productivity 30% and product quality 20%.
- Reduced margin cost of business unit operations $11 million by initiating key process improvement systems.
- Designed and led transition of several acquisitions from vertical business units to functional organization structure resulting in more efficient utilization of resources and improved operational performance.

Consulting
- Led launch and development of industry-leading consulting firm from conception to a four-division enterprise. Instrumental in reducing costs while concurrently increasing efficiency for numerous Fortune 500 and 1000 companies by developing and implementing wide scale organizational and human resources initiatives.
- Designed and led reorganization initiatives resulting in annual savings of $1.4 million.
- Reduced costs $5 million for a client organization by leading development of key processes and procedures to shift focus to incremental margins.

PROFESSIONAL EXPERIENCE

White Ridge Energy	Huntington, WV	2004-present
Director, Human Resources		
Jenkins Cooper, LTD	Tucson, AZ	2001-2004
Corporate Director, Organizational Effectiveness		
Center for Creative Management, Inc. St. Louis, MO	1989 – 2001	
President		

EDUCATION AND TRAINING

ABA University, Albuquerque, New Mexico
Master of Business Administration (MBA); Human Resources Management

Craig University, Stowe, Vermont
Bachelor of Arts (BA) • Psychology & Philosophy
CMC Certification in Human Resources, Institute of Management Consultant, Washington, D.C.

Example 2-3

JOHN P. HESER
2703 Maple Place, Harrisburg, IL 618-555-1212

PROFILE
Administration * Management

Results focused administrator with a notable record of success in management, administration, sales, customer service and performance management. Astute change leader able to provide direction and tactical execution of business strategy. Top ranked administrator highly qualified in the planning, development and management of organizational initiatives. Strong background in sales, public administration, customer service and credit/collections. Persuasive consensus builder adapt in cross-functional negotiations to achieve "win-win" outcomes.

Core Competencies:

*Administration	*Decision Analysis	*Project Management
*Performance Management	*Supervision	*Organizational Renewal
*Public Relations	*Sales	*Problem Solving
*Credit & Collections	*Accounting	*Customer Service
*Compensation	*Performance Management	*Real Estate Law

KEY ACHIEVEMENTS

*Determined and resourceful performer who consistently achieves organizational goals by reducing internal project preparation costs by 15% annually.

*Established problem prevention program to address financial concerns of parents that reduced customer complaints by 30%

*Developed conflict management strategy that settled over 55% of delinquent accounts before moving to out sourced collection agency.

*Created a customer service program that reduced in-process accounting activity by 40%.

*Developed the initial University endowment program leading to more sophisticated fundraising activity thus increasing bottom line returns by 30%.

*Developed and streamlined approach to the evaluation of admissions requirements, saving 20% of in process costs equaling 3 million dollars in savings per year.

*Reduced admissions process time by 30% and project workload by 20% by implementing new systematic approach to University Admissions.

*Brought in from Tarkio College to Chesnut University as a member of the turnaround team charged with organization renewal activity that brought the University from the brink of bankruptcy with a student population of less than 450 students into a thriving organization in 5 years.

*Designed processes and internal programs that aligned with organizational goals that built the student population from 450 to 15,000 students in 12 years.

PROFESSIONAL EXPERIENCE

CHESTER & SWARTZ CONSULTANTS– Harrisburg, IL (2002-Present) Project Development - responsible for overseeing multiple projects in a multi-disciplined consulting organization.

COLDWELL BANKER – St. Charles, MO (2003-Present) <u>Real Estate Executive</u> – responsible for sales, service, customer relations and administrative management in an environment that places major emphasis in both residential sales performance and commercial real estate development opportunities.

CHESTNUT UNIVERSITY – St. Louis, MO (1989-2002) Private University serving the educational needs of a student body of nearly 15,000 at 4 locations offering over 100 degreed programs for both traditional and nontraditional students.

<u>Business Office Administrator</u> 1994-2002 – Managed and monitored domestic student account activity. Managed domestic and international financial records, credit and collection practices and Business Office customer service activity. University liaison with International community in collection of off-shore student account indebtedness. Responsible for university work and learn programs.
<u>Office Manager – Development</u> (1993-1994) Initiated and implemented a list of fundraising activities that produced multi-million dollar returns.
<u>Office Manager – Evening and Graduate School Admissions</u> (1991-1993) Managed student admissions process, coordinated student profiles for evaluation of admissions requirements. Supervised University work-study staff.
<u>Director of Student Life</u> (1989-1991) Developed and directed the University work and learn program for all campus students. Responsible for University student housing and campus ID record system. Arranged all campus social activities.

PRIOR EXPERIENCE includes: Management (student activity and athletics, Tarkio College). Management (Upward Bound Program, Morehead State University). Business Owner, Automobile Dealership and Pallet Manufacturing Company, Georgetown, Ohio.

EDUCATION

Morehead State University, Morehead, KY. MBA Business Management

University of Breckenridge, Johnson City Oklahoma, BA., Psychology

State of Missouri Real Estate Board and Certification

ACHIEVEMENTS AND NOTABLE DISTINCTIONS

Illinois Business Advisory Council (2003-2005)

PROFESSIONAL AFFILIATIONS

American Management Association (2001-2004)

American Association of Business Administrators (2002-2004)

A Simple Twist to Your Resume May Further Entice the Reader

Remember that your goal is to get that interview. This is accomplished by positioning yourself above your competition. Each and every line of your resume must be written to "inspire" the reader to continue.

Some hiring officers have actually stated that a simple adjustment in the resume structure could make it an even more compelling read.

As you develop your professional summary for the positions you held over your employment history, you may wish to arrange your accomplishments in a manner that describes the challenges that you faced in each position, followed by a series of results and accomplishments that you achieved to meet those challenges. By demonstrating this challenge/results relationship you show the resume reader that you possess the skills and talents that they are seeking. The following example demonstrates the process:

Company Name and brief description

Position: Director of HR   2004 to Present

Challenge: To create an HR infrastructure that would better support business growth, be more customer responsive and reduce internal business costs.

Results: Re-branded the HR function and established the department as a strategic business partner aligning HR objectives to corporate goals.

Developed and implemented short and long term HR strategies, revised policy and procedure, business systems that positively impacted all human capital via ease of use.

Re-negotiated a cost effective corporate benefits program that reduced overall company benefits administration costs by $9M dollars annually.

You should include a series of challenge/results for each position you held in your chronology resume. By listing your results and achievements in this manner, the reader is more capable of relating to the skills that you bring to the table.

Rules of the Road When Constructing Your Resume

- Always omit your previous salary.
- Keep the resume limited to two pages, but not more than three pages maximum if you have extensive experience to share.
- Use proper grammar, spelling and punctuation.
- Focus on the best content and present your resume in the most convincing manner.

- Demonstrate in the resume that you are flexible and upwardly mobile.
- When placing dates, use full years only (i.e., 1993-2002).
- In all resumes, save some room for honors, awards, certifications, patents, and licenses. It shows achievement.
- Remember that most industries have their own "language." Research the industry and use some of that language in your resume.
- Never include your social security number.
- Design your resume to be tasteful and understandable.
- Do not include references; you will provide them later.
- Always place your name and the page number at the top of your resume for all pages beyond the first.
- Be sure that your resume is <u>not</u> over inflated or dishonest.
- Pass your resume out to friends in order to gain feedback. Take their ideas seriously and incorporate them into the document if you feel it makes sense.

Your Elevator Speech

Once your resume has been completed and you feel comfortable with the product you developed, you will also need to develop what is known as an "elevator speech." This is a verbal promotional pitch that you present to others featuring key information about you. Generally speaking, this verbal presentation should take no more than three minutes to deliver. The elevator speech is used most during one-on-one meetings, such as telephone and/or face-to-face interviews or in the event someone asks you to share your professional experiences.

Six Rules for Creating Your Elevator Speech

1. Divide your speech into two parts: 1) your work history and selected accomplishments; 2) what you are seeking in a new position.
2. Front load your presentation with information about what you would bring to the table.
3. Make the presentation something that you can commit to memory.
4. Use language people can understand.
5. Develop the speech in a conversational style rather than a long-winded oratory.
6. When appropriate, hit the critical words that are part of the vocabulary for the industry you are targeting.

On the next page you will find a worksheet that you may use to develop your own elevator speech. Should you need assistance developing your pitch, you will find an example on page 27. As you develop your presentation, remember that it is your time to "toot your own horn," so make your presentation hard hitting and explosive.

Your Elevator Speech

WORKSHEET 2-4

- **Name:** _____
- **Previous Employment and Position Held:** _____
  _____
- **Selected Responsibilities in the Position:** _____
  _____
- **3 Areas of Achievement:** _____
  _____
- **3 Areas of Expertise:** _____
  _____
- **Your Education and Credentials:** _____
  _____
- **What You Are Seeking in the Future:** _____
  _____

Example 2-5   **Elevator Speech**

My name is Sam Jones. Most recently I was the Director of Human Resources for XYZ Manufacturing Corporation, the nation's largest privately held farming implement manufacturer. I drove all aspects of HR for the organization, spanning four manufacturing facilities and 3,000 employees with ten direct, and 34 indirect, reports.

A few of my achievements include: leading special projects that directly contributed to a 6% reduction in company costs; overhauled HR to create a state of the art, best in class operation that aligned with organizational business plans, and saved $7M in margin costs by initiating a Six Sigma program and employee engagement activity that fostered employee participation in the workplace.

My strengths include workplace culture reforms, designing total rewards systems, and performance management initiatives.

I hold a BA in Business Administration from Southern Illinois University and an MBA in Human Resources Management from Lindenwood University, with SPHR and Six Sigma Certifications.

I am seeking a position as an HR executive in a mid-sized organization where I can use my talents and skills to reduce costs and effect bottom line results.

CHAPTER 3: LETTER WRITING PART OF A WELL ORCHESTRATED JOB SEARCH CAMPAIGN

A portion of your personal marketing plan in combination with the resume and elevator speech will require you to construct letters of correspondence. From the cover letter used in conjunction with your resume, to thank-you and post interview letters, it is a good idea to have a few standardized letters in your portfolio that can be modified to meet your specific needs.

Out of the many letters that you will write, there are five key letters that are included as examples in this chapter:

- The Cover Letter For Your Resume
- The T-letter When Responding to Ads or used as Cover Letters
- The Thank-you Letter
- The Post Interview Letter (2 examples)
- The Thank You Letter after a Personal Telephone Call

<u>Some rules to follow when constructing your letters</u>

- Remember that your letters should be business-like, so watch the grammar, sentence structure, and spelling errors.
- Be certain to correctly spell the name of the person you are contacting. There's nothing worse than sending a letter of appreciation with an incorrectly spelled name.
- Use appropriate stationary for formal letters, or you may use e-mail or thank you cards to convey your message. Stay away from e-mails when you can.
- Always keep copies of your correspondence.

The Cover Letter

The Cover Letter is important because it expresses your sincerity and enthusiasm for the position you are seeking. The cover letter should generally be no more than three to four paragraphs in length and should convey to the reader the contribution you would make to the organization. Although in many cases you will respond to a "blind" job ad that does not reveal the name of the company officer involved in the job search, always attempt to find out (via company web page) the name of the HR director and address your cover letter accordingly. Try to stay away from "To Whom It May Concern" or "Dear Hiring Officer"" if possible find out the name. The following example represents a well constructed letter.

Example 3-1

JOHN L. SHOOTS

327 Johnson Court * Bronxville, NY 10708 * (H) 914-654-3277* **J.Shoots@email.com**

Date

Recipients Name
Title
Company
City, State, Zip

Dear_____:

As an experienced HR manager with OD proficiency, I have a superlative record of developing and implementing corporate-wide plans and programs that seamlessly dovetail with both short- and long-term organizational goals. Over the course of my career, I have honed my skills as both an HR consultant and full-time corporate HR leader to provide world-class strategies and tactics for Fortune 1000 and 500 companies spanning a broad range of industries. My value is illustrated by a history of effectively managing staff and employee relations while improving employee satisfaction levels and reducing attrition while significantly elevating bottom-line metrics.

My "big picture" perspective of organizational and marketplace dynamics has enabled me to create successful responses to new challenges, drive initiatives that improve employee performance while reducing costs, and recruit / develop top-level human capital to support company vision and goals. My broad, in-depth areas of expertise include project / program management, turnaround/start-up leadership, policy and procedure development, financial management, and succession planning.

I am confident that I can leverage my expertise and successes to provide significant value to your organization, and look forward to arranging a time to discuss how I can help you achieve your business objectives.

Sincerely,

John L. Shoots

Enclosure: resume

A Pledge of Commitment

Another way to differentiate you from the rest of the job applicants seeking the position is to enhance your cover letter with a pledge to your potential employer. This pledge is a written performance commitment statement that describes your future potential and the value you bring to the position you are seeking. The pledge may be structured as a portion of the cover letter as follows:

As a candidate for this position I pledge my total commitment and dedication in support of your bottom line objectives and organizational growth by .... (In this space you would expand upon the specific strengths that you would immediately bring to the hiring organization.)

By adding a pledge statement to the text of your cover letter you demonstrate to the hiring officer your commitment to make an immediate and lasting contribution.

Use of the T-Letter

The T-Letter may also be used as a cover letter in support of your resume. It offers the recruiter or hiring officer an opportunity to review your specific qualifications that directly relate to the job requirements. The T-letter may also be used to answer newspaper ads, job boards, and other position listings. This format is a means of stirring interest and encourages the reader to seek more information about you. An example follows on the next page.

Example 3-2

JOHN L. SHOOTS

822 Johnson Court * Bronxville, NY 10705(H) 314-654-3277 * J. Shoots@email.com

Date

Recipient's NameTitle
Company
City, State, Zip

Dear _____:

It is with a great deal of interest and enthusiasm that I submit my resume to you for the position of Senior HR Business Partner. As a seasoned HR strategist, I have a superlative record of developing and implementing corporate-wide HR plans and programs that seamlessly dovetail with both short and long-term organizational programs that significantly elevate bottom-line metrics. Highlights of my qualifications include:

Your Requirements	My Qualifications
*HR Executive with 10 years of Generalist experience	*HR Executive with 15+ years of experience in all matters of Human Resources leadership
*Broad background in Organizational Development	*10+ years of OD experience with a solid track record in aligning OD initiatives with corporate objectives
*Bachelor's degree in business, human resources or related field	*Hold MBA in Organizational Behavior
*PHR Certification required	*Possess SPHR and CPCM Certification
*Knowledge of Microsoft Office including Word, Excel, Access, Outlook and Power Point	*Have full knowledge in the use of all Microsoft office products
*Excellent employee relations and coaching skills coaching	*10+ years of employee relations responsibility and skills while Director of HR with XYZ Organization

I am confident in my ability and expertise to provide significant value to your organization and look forward to arranging a time to discuss how I can help you achieve your business objectives.

Sincerely,

John L. Shoots

Enclosed – Resume

Example 3-3

The Thank You Letter

The thank you letter is also important to the success of your campaign. This letter can be used for all sorts of acknowledgements. Keep the letter short and to the point. Show the person that you truly appreciate their kindness. An example follows.

Thank You Letter after a Personal Meeting

Sample

Jane M. Monroe

111 Marilyn St. * Washington, Delaware * 12202 *201-555-1212 * j.monroe@yahoo.com

Date:

Recipient Name
Title
Company
Address
City, State, Zip

Dear _____,

Thank you for the insight you provided me yesterday during our meeting. Your specific suggestions and ideas about the future needs and opportunities in the truckload transportation industry will be of great help. I particularly enjoyed your thoughts regarding the new trends that you are currently experiencing and the skill sets people will be required to have for the future.

Per your suggestion, I plan to contact Sam Jones this week from XYZ Transportation to arrange a meeting. If you don't mind, I would like to use your name as a way of introduction.

Best Wishes,

Jane M. Monroe

Example 3-4

The Post Interview Letter #1

After taking part in the interview it is important to continue to show your interest in the position. Since the interviewer will probably be interviewing others for the position the post interview letter will keep your name out front and in the running. This letter should go directly to the responsible interviewer. Here is one example of a post interview letter:

SAMPLE

THOMAS J. SNEED

10 Long Branch Rd. * Dixie, MI, 20222 (H) 200-455-7879 * t.sneed@yahoo.com

Date

Recipient Name
Title
Company
Address
City, State, Zip

Dear _____,

It was a pleasure to have met with you yesterday to discuss the role of the position of Director of Organizational Development.

I would like to reiterate my strong interest in the position and enthusiasm in working with people like you that are truly dedicated to the success of the business. To facilitate your decision-making I would like to review a few of my qualifications:

- Fifteen plus years of successful results providing strategic direction in talent management and operational effectiveness initiatives that drives profitability, promotes organizational growth, and reduces corporate risk.
- Expert senior level consultant in developing organizational effectiveness initiatives and business strategies that contributes directly to the bottom line.
- Broad background in operational efficiency, six-sigma process improvement, proactive employee relations, change leadership, talent management and leadership development.
- Functional expert in learning development, adult learning systems, curriculum development, and educational delivery approaches.
- Experienced in industrial manufacturing with a solid background in process management and organizational growth models.

Thank you for the opportunity to meet with you. I look forward to hearing from you soon.

Sincerely,

Thomas J. Sneed

Here is a second example of the Post Interview Letter that maybe used.

Example 3-5

The Post Interview Letter #2

THOMAS J. SNEED

10 Long Branch Rd. * Dixie, MI, 20222   (H) 200-455-7879 * T.Sneed@email.com

Date

Recipient Name
Title
Company
Address
City, State, Zip

Dear _____,

It was a pleasure to have met you yesterday to discuss the Director of Engineering position. I would like to reiterate my interest in the position and sincere enthusiasm in working with people like you that are truly committed to the success of the business.

Per your explanation of the position and in discussing my skills and abilities, I am confident that I would add value to the position and to the organization.

Thank you for the opportunity to meet with you. I look forward to hearing from you soon.

Sincerely,

Thomas J. Sneed

Thank You Letter after Personal Telephone Call

As a matter of courtesy, the thank you letter after a personal telephone call indicates to the recipient your professionalism and sincerity. A example follows:

Example 3-6

Jane M. Monroe

111 Marilyn St. * Washington, Delaware * 12202 * 201-555-1212 * J.Monroe@email.com

Date

Recipient Name
Title
Company
Address
City, State, Zip

Dear _____,

I wish to thank you for taking time to speak with me about the XYZ industry and the opportunities you see for an individual with my background and experience. Sharing your knowledge and expertise with me is greatly appreciated.

I plan to contact Mr. LLL per your suggestion with the hope that he can provide me with additional information about the industry. If you don't mind, I would like to use your name as a way of introduction.

Best Wishes,

Jane M. Monroe

These example letters will enable you to structure your own messages to meet your specific needs.

CHAPTER 4: THE INTERVIEWING PROCESS

Now that you've completed your resume, your elevator speech, and have developed your collection of written correspondence, let's move to the interview itself.

To help you better understand the use of the interview in your job search, we will first describe the sequential steps that are generally used by company hiring officers when selecting and placing a candidate. Known in Human Resources terms as the "hiring chronology," you will find that the interview is linked to a whole series of events that is intended to provide the total picture of a job candidate. Let's take a look.

The Hiring Chronology

Step 1 – The Company conducts a position needs assessment, which is an evaluation of job requirements and skill sets, in order to design an updated job description for the position vacancy.

Step 2 - An internal search for candidates to fill the position is conducted (promotion from within).

Step 3 - A review of internal candidates for qualifications that match the position requirements is conducted.

Step 4 - If the internal candidate list proves unsuccessful, a search for external candidates begins (advertise for position vacancy).

Step 5 - Resumes and applications from external candidates are received and screened for qualifications match. On some occasions telephone calls are made to certain candidates to review and verify specific portions of the resume requiring clarification.

Step 6 – Once the application/resume screening step is completed, the company conducts screening interviews with selected external candidates. If you are a local candidate and have been considered, the interview will generally be a face-to-face event. On some occasions, however, instead of going to the company location, you may be asked to participate in a telephone interview or internet webcam screening instead. This is done as a cost savings should the candidate live a great distance from the company location.

At this point in the process, candidates are generally required to complete a formal company application. Once again, should you live a great distance from the company and participate in the telephone interview, you may be asked to complete the application electronically/online.

<u>Step 7</u> – The Company will now conduct reference checks and background investigations on those successful external candidates that have moved past the screening interview phase.

<u>Step 8</u> –Those candidates that have successfully moved past the reference check and background investigation phase will participate in the placement interview. It is at this phase when compensation and benefits are discussed.

There are those occasions when two or more candidates have successfully interviewed during the placement interview phase. Should this happen another interview may be required to make the final placement determination. Generally, a new group of interviewers will participate in the process.

<u>Step 9</u> – A final candidate is then selected by the hiring manager, subject to the passing of a company physical, if required.

<u>Step 10</u> – If the physical is passed, a telephone call is made to inform the candidate of the results and an offer letter is sent that reflects and reinforces the terms of the position.

<u>Step 11</u> – The candidate accepts the position in writing and company on-boarding and orientation is arranged.

The Screening Interview

As you see from the Hiring Chronology you will generally need to participate in more than one interview before landing that new position. The initial interview is known as the screening interview and is generally conducted by Human Resources. This interview will determine whether or not you will be invited back to participate in a second interview. The screening interview usually focuses upon the technical competency required of the position along with work history and the reasons for leaving previous employers, so have your answers ready. Always remember that the hiring organization is seeking a candidate that is a solid match. Speak in terms of what you can do for the company.

The Placement Interview

If you pass the screening interview, you will be invited to participate in the placement interview. This interview will always be a face-to-face encounter, no matter your traveling distance. You will either be asked to come to the business location or a mutually agreeable location will be chosen for the interview.

The placement interview may be conducted by the hiring manager only, or you may be asked to first participate in a panel interview with other managers and staff personnel with whom you would be working. A final interview with the hiring manager concludes the process.

The interviewers already know of your technical competency and job qualifications after the debriefing from the screening interviewer, so the focus of the placement interview is dedicated to learning more about your compatibility, competency, accomplishments, and future job potential.

Interviewer Styles

During the interview, you will likely experience various interviewing styles. Styles you may encounter include:

The Interrogator – The interviewer exhibiting this style asks specific questions in rapid succession that will require you to answer with short, specific answers. These questions can usually be answered with simple yes or no responses.

The Reporter – This interviewing style asks questions that generally begin with what, where, who, when, why, and how. The reporter style encourages the candidate to provide more detailed information rather than providing short abbreviated answers.

The Prober – The Prober will ask a question, and after an answer is provided, will ask a second question requiring the candidate to provide even more detailed information about the initial question.

The Behaviorist – This interviewing style is designed to structure questions around situations that the candidate has faced in his/her work history. These questions generally begin with, "Tell me about a time when you . . . ."

The Pontificator – This interviewer does the majority of the talking, mainly about him- or herself.

No matter the style, <u>be prepared to answer the questions presented to you</u>. Remember, prior preparation is everything!

Don't Be Intimidated by the Interview Process

We've been raised in a society where we were told that it was impolite to talk about ourselves. However, during an interview this is a requirement, and you are to talk about yourself in front of complete strangers who will be evaluating what you say. Talk about pressure!

Like players on a stage, there will likely be "opening night jitters," but the key to an actor's success is in knowing his lines. This requires practice and preparation. The more practice, the greater the confidence.

The same holds true for the interview. Learn your lines by reviewing your resume and the answers you will provide to those tested questions found later in this book. Be natural, be yourself, and answer each question to the best of your ability. If you are uncertain what is being asked of you by the interviewer, don't be afraid to have the question repeated.

Before the interview, review your personal accomplishments, work history, and the responses you provided in the Worksheets found in Chapter 1. Be able to explain the actions you took when you accomplished the great achievements you listed on your resume.

By the same token, you may also be asked about a time when the end result you achieved was not what you had intended. When providing your answer, turn the negative into a positive by telling the interviewer what you learned from the experience and how you applied the learning in another, similar, situation.

It is the responsibility of the interviewer to conduct a well orchestrated interview so that information can be collected quickly, and in a pleasant, unthreatening environment. Don't attempt to carry the interview should you find an interviewer lacking skills. Be patient, maintain your professionalism, and provide the information required. As a general rule, the interviewer will be doing twenty percent of the talking while the candidate will be speaking the remaining eighty percent.

To assist you in better understanding the flow of the interview and what you might expect as a job candidate, the next sections provide an overview of the interview process and the types of questions usually asked.

The Interview

An effective interview usually follows a format that:
- Allows the interviewer to control the flow of the discussion.
- Allows the interviewer to obtain enough information to formulate a decision or conclusion about the candidate and his qualifications.
- Avoids the use of illegal questions.
- Allows the candidate to ask questions about the position being filled.
- Puts the company in a positive light.

The interview consists of three phases:
- <u>The Introduction</u> – You are greeted and welcomed. The interviewer clarifies the purpose for the meeting and what you can expect during the interview. In some cases you may be asked to meet with other people. If that is the case, a schedule of activity is generally provided to you.
- <u>The Body</u> – You will be expected to provide information about your work history, education, experiences, personal characteristics, and attributes through a series of well-thought-out questions. This is generally accomplished in a

relaxed conversational manner where both you and the interviewer exchange information.

- <u>The Closing</u> – The interviewer answers any questions that you might have, sells the job and company, if appropriate, and tells you what the next step will be. If the next step is not revealed to you, don't be afraid to ask.

The interview has a twofold purpose:

- To obtain enough information to select the candidate that best matches the job requirements and will work well with other department members.
- To determine with great accuracy the individual that will perform best in the future.

Interviewers generally develop and ask questions that provide information in six key areas, as demonstrated in the box below.

• Intellectual skills and aptitudes	• Motivational needs and values
• Personality strengths and attributes	• Knowledge and experience
• Work history	• Future potential

At the conclusion of the interview a good interviewer should be capable of writing a paragraph about you, the candidate. The questions the interviewer asks and the answers that you provide will determine the sum total of the information gathered to construct the descriptive paragraph. Your role is to emphasize the information you want the interviewer to remember.

Questioning During the Interview

The sophistication of the interviewer will generally determine the questions that will be asked. You may be asked some very simple questions that require a mere yes or no response. Other questions may be more complex and will test your thought processes. Behaviorally based questions are always the roughest, for they require you to think through an answer using real life examples, experiences, and situations. Let's look at a few examples of behaviorally based questions.

Typical Behaviorally Based Questions

This line of questioning found below provides the interviewer with a great deal of information about you, how you think, how you present your ideas, and, in general, tests your ability to formulate logical conclusions.

<u>Evaluation of leadership</u>

Question: Tell me about a time when you encountered an employee that did not want to follow your instructions.

Follow-up Question: Where was it? How did you handle the situation? What was the outcome?

<u>Evaluation of problem solving skills</u>

Question: Tell me about one of the most difficult problems you faced on your last job.

Follow-up Question: Why was it difficult? How did you handle it? What was the outcome?

<u>Evaluation of accomplishments</u>

Question: Tell me about your greatest personal achievement in your career.

Follow-up Question: Why was it so important? What was the result?

<u>Evaluation of the application of technical job skills</u>

Question: Tell me how you would evaluate any changes you would make when you first take over the position.

Follow-up Question: Why would you do it that way?

Questions That May Be Asked

Your resume already provides a great deal of information about you, so most savvy interviewers will construct a series of questions that will provide information outside the scope of your resume. To help you further prepare for the interview, a series of other frequently asked questions that interviewers may use is provided:

Communications

- What are some instances when you've had to market yourself to someone else?
- What does it take to express an idea to others?
- Can you tell me about situations where you have seen others use particularly poor techniques in order to get their ideas across to others? What types of techniques were they?
- What was the toughest idea you had to "sell" to your boss? Did he buy the idea?
- What do you feel are your strengths when communicating with others?

Creativity and Conceptualization

- What kinds of tasks do you feel are the most difficult for you to execute?
- What tasks give you the greatest satisfaction?
- What frustrates you the most and how do you deal with it?
- What changes have you made in your approach to others that demonstrate your adaptability in a work setting?

Teamwork

- What types of people do you like to work with?
- What do you think are the best ways of building teamwork?
- What kind of people do you find it most difficult to work with? Why?
- Do you prefer working alone or in groups?
- What qualities do you look for in the people who work for you? With you?
- What types of situations do you like to avoid getting involved with?

Potential Leadership Abilities

- What jobs have you had in the organizations you have belonged to?
- What types of people do you especially respect? Why?
- What do you think are the qualities of a good leader?
- What do you think are the major problems facing management today?
- How do you like to be supervised?
- What are some of the things about which you and your supervisor might disagree? How should this conflict be handled?
- Do you have any positions of authority or leadership in your current job? How do you perform in these positions?
- What are some of the things that your boss did with which you were particularly pleased? Not pleased?
- What have you found to be most effective in maintaining discipline among subordinates?
- How do you interpret the word "delegation"?
- Can you give me an example or two of your abilities to supervise others?

Ambition

- What are your long term career goals?
- What are some of the things you want to accomplish?
- Who/what in your life would you say influenced you the most in regard to these goals and objectives?
- What personal characteristics might make you successful?
- What in your experience suits you for our kind of work?
- Would you want to stay within your specialty or do you foresee using it as a stepping stone into management?
- If you could do (be) anything you wanted what would you do (be)?
- What would you say motivates you?
- In what ways do you feel you have grown in the past 2 to 3 years?

Accomplishments / Abilities

- What have you done in school, at work, or in your community that you are most proud of?
- What recognition have you gotten from your work, community, schooling, hobbies, or military experience?
- What would you consider to be your greatest achievement to date? Why?
- In what areas of work do you do your best?
- What are some of the problems you encountered in your past job and which of these frustrates you the most? What did you usually do about it?
- How do you feel your boss rates your work performance?
- What were some of the things that your boss indicated you could improve upon? What action did you take?
- What qualities about yourself do you believe account for your being considered for this position?
- What activities or accomplishments give you the greatest satisfaction?
- Do you consider yourself a self starter?
- In what ways have you made yourself a more effective person?

Adaptability

- What are some of the things you want to avoid in future jobs?
- Are you willing to relocate?
- Are there any geographic areas or work situations that you would particularly wish to avoid?
- If given a preference in working in a highly urbanized or remote location, which would you prefer? Why?

Projected Work Stability

- Do you want to stay in your specialty or use it as a stepping stone to something else? What would that be? Why?
- What kinds of job pressures bother you most?
- Most jobs have positives and negatives. What are some of the positives/negatives in your current or previous job?
- What do you see as the primary positives and negatives in pursuing a career with us?
- Do you prefer a job with a variety of tasks or one with a set routine?
- What would you say is the most important thing you are looking for in an employer?
- How do you feel about travel? On the average, how many nights would you be willing to be away from home?

- Are you willing to work overtime or have your time off on days other than Saturday and Sunday?
- How do you feel about working holidays if needed?

Interpersonal Skills (IPS)

- What do you do when you have trouble with a colleague?
- If there are problems with a supervisor, do you speak up for what you believe in?
- How would you characterize your personality?
- In dealing with people, what kinds of things do you feel most confident in doing?
- Give me three words that best describe you.
- How would you handle a complaint or compliment?
- What is the one thing that people do that most annoys you?

Overall Impression

- Why should we hire you over other job applicants?
- What are you looking for from us?
- What do you feel, you can do for us?

Your Objective During the Interview

Look at the interview as a buy/sell arrangement. Your objective as a job candidate is to show the interviewer (the buyer) that you are capable of filling the position requirements. You are "selling" yourself, so be certain to present yourself in such a way that you convince the interviewer that you possess the experience, skills, and abilities that are essential for the position. Be positive, upbeat, convincing and confident in the answers that you provide.

Once you've successfully accomplished your sales objective, the interviewer will then begin to present the company and the job in a very positive light. You now become the buyer and the interviewer becomes the seller. It is now your opportunity to ask pertinent questions about the position. Below, you will find a list of appropriate questions for your interviewer.

Typical questions you should ask include:
- To whom does this position report?
- Why is the position open?
- What are the lines of authority and responsibility in this position?
- What made the previous employee successful in this position? Where is s/he today?
- Tell me more about the workplace culture.
- What does XYZ Company have over its competitors?
- What are the budgetary responsibilities of the position?

- How are people currently being evaluated?
- Is there anything in my background that would indicate I couldn't do an outstanding job here at XYZ Company? If so, what are they?
- What specific qualities do you feel are important to this position?
- Are there any indications of expansion or acquisition that will grow the business in the near future?
- What are the immediate challenges for the person in this role?
- Is this a new position or a job vacancy?
- I am very impressed in what I have heard so far and am very interested in this opportunity. What is the next step?

First Impressions Count

Your first impression is the most important statement you can make about yourself. How you appear and what you are wearing will be the first judgment of the interviewer. The candidate that is dressed in a business suit and tie or sports jacket and golf shirt will make a better impression than the individual wearing blue jeans and T-shirt. If you dress for success then you will appear successful.

One way to be sure of your wardrobe selection for the interview is to ASK. When contacted for the interview, feel free to ask about the dress code and prepare accordingly. Even if you are seeking a manufacturing or mining position in a traditionally dirty setting, don't fall into the trap of under-dressing for the interview. Putting your best foot forward is important. But remember, you don't have to spend a million bucks to look like it!

Men's Attire:
- Suit (solid color – dark grey or navy
- Clean pressed shirt
- Tie in subtle colors to match your suit
- Belt that matches your shoe color
- Dark socks to match your suit pants
- Dress shoes (polished); no sneakers
- Little or no jewelry
- Clean hair
- Minimal cologne or none at all
- Clean hands and nails
- Briefcase with pen, note pad, and extra resumes

Women's Attire:
- Suit (dark grey, navy, or black); if a skirt suit, skirt should be no shorter than 2" above the knee
- Clean pressed blouse; not low cut
- Dress shoes (polished); no spiked heels
- Clean hair

- Minimal perfume and make-up
- Clean hands and nails
- Briefcase with pen, note pad and extra resumes

In some areas of the United States business casual is also acceptable attire. This includes:

Men's Attire:
- Clean pressed shirt/sweater
- Sports jacket
- Clean and pressed slacks
- Belt
- Clean color matched socks that complements the sports jacket
- Polished shoes or boots

Women's Attire:
- Clean pressed blouse
- Skirt or Slacks (dark gray or navy)
- Polished shoes (flats or short heels)

Things not to bring to an Interview
- Beverages
- Chewing gum/candy
- Cell phone
- Excess jewelry; women should limit earrings to one set and men should remove all earrings.
- Cover all visible tattoos
- Mp3 player

After completing either the screening or placement interview it is important to put down in writing your thoughts about the experience. See this as a critique of the interviewing process and how well you felt you performed.

Example 4-1

Post Interview Notes and Thoughts

Company_____

Interviewer's Name_____

Position Interviewed for: _____

Position of Interviewer_____

Date _____

- What did you like best about the interviewing process you experienced?

- Were you well received by the receptionist?

- Was the interviewer well prepared?

- How well do you feel you performed in the interview?

- Were you prepared for the interview?

- Areas for your personal improvement:

- Areas where you performed well:

- What questions did you have the most trouble answering?

- What questions did you answer well?

- What would you do differently in your next interview?

- What would you do again?

- If this was a screening interview, did the interviewer indicate the possibility of a call back? Did s/he indicate when?

- If the interviewer did not mention a call back, did you take the initiative and ask about the next step? What was the interviewer's response?

CHAPTER 5: DEVELOPING YOUR ACTION PLAN AND RECORD KEEPING SYSTEMS

The importance of being prepared for every step of the job search **before** executing an action plan cannot be over-emphasized. Should you fail to learn and execute the key preparation steps first, you are assured of making critical mistakes that will be costly to your landing the position you seek. It is for this reason that we took you through the essential steps before you develop the action plan.

Thus far, we have covered the following:

- Seeking a new job opportunity – getting mentally ready.
- Developing a process for self exploration and information gathering to support the construction of your resume and the targeting of your job search.
- Constructing the resume.
- The use of written correspondence to capture and maintain the interest of others.
- Putting your best foot forward during the interviewing process.

With this knowledge, you can now construct an action plan that will move your campaign forward. The action plan is the strategy required to properly market the product. That product is you!

Begin Your Action Plan - Start Networking

Networking is the ability to find and connect with people that will assist you in your job search and is the source of over seventy percent of new hires. To begin your networking, start with e-mails and telephone contacts to let friends and former associates know that you are currently in transition and seeking a new job opportunity. Remember that people you know may know others who can be of immediate assistance to you. Target those specific individuals who have access to individuals who have the type of job leads that you need. Your goal is to seek exposure and high visibility during this time.

If you are directed by a friend to telephone someone that he knows and you don't, use a **letter of introduction** first. Most executives don't have a lot of time to speak with strangers, so this form of initial contact will eliminate surprises. Always use the name of the individual suggesting the referral contact in the text of your letter. Review the following example for suggestions on how to format a letter of introduction.

Letter of Introduction

Example 5-1

JERRY P. LEWIS

1212 Holly Lane * Tangle Wood, LA 45032(H) 890-855-4953 * <u>J.Lewis@email.com</u>

Date

Recipient Name
Title
Company
Address
City, State, Zip

Dear _____,

Most recently my position with the XYZ Company was among those eliminated as the firm went through a reorganization and reduction in force.

I am currently seeking employment opportunities and thought it best to contact executives in the area. My friend Tom Jones, a former colleague of yours suggested that I send my resume to you for review. I am not asking for a position, just an opportunity to get your thoughts about the employment picture in the region with the hope that you could offer suggestions or provide the names of others that could be of assistance to me in my position search.

I would like to telephone you next Tuesday, January 23rd between 9am and 11am to arrange a convenient date and time for us to speak. I would appreciate twenty minutes of your time.

I wish to thank you in advance for any information you could provide.

Sincerely,

Jerry Lewis

Enclosure: Resume

Use of the Individual Telephone Worksheet

The more you network by telephone, the greater the need to record your telephone information for future use. Before sending letters to prospective telephone contacts, take time to develop a suitable telephone contact record. We've developed a worksheet on page 53 that will assist you in two ways. First, the worksheet will help you structure your telephone conversation and organize your thoughts before making the call. Second, you will be able to record pertinent information from the telephone conversation after the call has been completed.

Portions of this worksheet should be completed before the telephone call is made. This will provide you with special notes and information you will use as talking points during your telephone discussion. Complete Sections A through E of the worksheet before making your call.

Once the call is completed, fill in Sections F and G. Be sure to follow-up with Section G immediately after the call. You will use one worksheet for each telephone call you make. Keep all completed worksheets in a three-ringed binder chronologically dated, most recent date appearing first in your binder.

The Individual Telephone Worksheet

Worksheet 5-2

Date: _____

A. Record name, title, company/organization, telephone number of the person you are contacting and name of person recommending the contact, if applicable.

_____

_____

B. Purpose of call: _____

_____

C. Your opening statement: _____

_____

_____

D. Questions you may have: _____

_____

_____

E. Your concluding remarks: _____

_____

_____

F. What you have learned during the telephone contact: _____

G. What action you will need to take or information to include in the thank you letter: _____

_____

General Telephone Log

A General Telephone Log is used to record <u>all</u> telephone calls that you've made. This will ensure that you've left no one out. Make certain that you also include the names of those people whom you contacted when using the Individual Telephone Worksheet on the previous page.

The log sheet is structured by column. After making the call, enter the information as follows:

- Column #1: Name of the contact and date
- Column #2: Contact number and business organization
- Column #3: Purpose for the contact
- Column #4: Name of the person that recommended the contact (if applicable)
- Column #5: Follow-up action required of you

GENERAL TELEPHONE LOG

WORKSHEET 5-3

Name of Contact Date of Contact	Contact #/Address Including Organization	Purpose for the Contact	Name of Person Who Recommended the Call	Action Required

The Use of Websites and Job Boards in Your Job Search

The use of Web Sites such as HR Ladder, 6 Figures, Execunet, Monster, and Hound, to name a few, list job openings from businesses and recruiters working on behalf of businesses across the country. These services offer you the opportunity to apply for positions of which you normally may not be aware.

Businesses and recruiters use websites to post job positions and requirements for eager candidates to view. The format is simple: the position title, location, industry, professional experience, responsibilities, and key competencies are posted. All you need to do is apply for the position electronically.

Consider job boards as a resource, but the chances of landing a position using this method are slim. Nevertheless, should you use this job board method, it is important to know that your resume must reflect, as closely as possible, the job skills and requirements requested in the posting. If it does not mirror the requirements, you may need to adapt and adjust your resume to meet the specific needs of the position. We also suggest that you use the same key words that were used in the job description and qualifications section. You will have a better chance of being recognized as a potential candidate if you do.

Final Word: Your best bet – **Network, Network, Network!!!!!**

Website Search Log

Should you submit your resume electronically, record this information on the Web Search Log. Note the date, website (Hound, Monster, etc.) the company name or name of the recruiter, industry, and position title. Should you receive an electronic notice from the company that they received your resume, mark "active" in the status column on the right and record the date you received the notice.

If in a few weeks you receive a reject notice, cross out "active" and write "inactive" in its place. Also, include the date of this transaction. If you are considered for the position, you will generally receive an email response or telephone contact with further instructions. This log will help you maintain accurate records of positions for which you have applied.

WEBSITE SEARCH LOG

WORKSHEET 5-4

DATE	WEB SITE	COMPANY/ RECRUITER	INDUSTRY	POSITION	STATUS/ DATE

Support Groups

A part of your job search action plan and networking strategy should also include participation in local support groups committed to assisting job seekers. These groups bring people together for the purpose of exchanging information and ideas. You may wish to contact the unemployment office or local community college outreach centers to see what groups are available in your community and when and where they meet.

The Weekly Planner

There is an old adage: "when you don't know where you're going, any road will take you there." Thus the reasoning behind the use of a weekly planner--it keeps you on track. See it as a weekly "to do" list. As you develop your plans and activities for the week ahead, record the actions you need to take on the form. Note the various letters you will need to send, telephone calls and responses to ads you will need to make, positions to which you wish to apply, meetings and professional gatherings you will attend, specific companies you wish to contact, and any scheduled interviews you may have. As you record your information on this weekly planner you will need to be specific. If you do your homework and record your information religiously, you will have a document that will work for you week after week. The next page provides the format to follow.

WEEKLY ACTIVITY PLANNER

WORKSHEET 5-5

Dates from_____ to _____

	Monday	Tuesday	Wednesday	Thursday	Friday	Saturday
Letters to Send						
To Whom						
Purpose of Letter						
Type of Letter						
Telephone Contacts to Make						
To Whom/ Company						
Telephone # Purpose						
Response to Ads						
Company/ Recruiter						
To Whom: Name						
Response to Job Boards						
Job Board Name						
Company/ Recruiter						
Job/Position						

Meetings to Attend					
Type of Event					
Where					
With Whom					
People Met					
Companies to Contact					
Reason for Contact					
Contact Person/ Company					
Telephone – Interviews					
Contact Person					
Status					
Interviews					
Screening/ Placement					
Contact Person					
Status of Interview					

Timing Is Everything

Generally speaking, the majority of time that you devote to the job search should be equal to or greater than the amount of time you spent on your previous job. If, for example, you worked eight hours per day, you should devote at least eight hours per day on your job search. In that eight hour period, not more than twenty percent of your time should be devoted to job boards. The remainder of your time should be devoted to networking, developing relationships, and letter writing.

Attitude Will Help You Succeed

The job marketplace suggests that by the end of this recession, job losses may exceed 10%. All we hear is gloom and doom, to the point that some people are giving up on the job search altogether. Don't give up! There are still success stories out there. Focus on your skills. Those things that made you successful in the past weren't driven by a good or bad economy; they were driven by the skills and experiences you brought to the workplace. Your skills, aptitudes, and abilities aren't left at the door when you leave a job. They are transportable – they go with you. Companies are still looking for talented people. Your job is to connect with the company that is looking for someone like you. Continue to believe in yourself.

CHAPTER 6: DISCUSSING COMPENSATION

Adiscussion on compensation with your potential employer is so important that we devoted this chapter to the subject. Discussions about compensation can be awkward if you don't know what to say or do when the subject is addressed. Generally speaking, talks of salary do not come about until the hiring organization is relatively certain of their interest in you.

For some positions there is no compensation flexibility due to prior contractual arrangements or government restrictions. In these situations the wage is pre-set for the position and cannot be altered or changed. If the compensation is not pre-set, there could be some flexibility in negotiating your salary.

Some hiring officers make it a "cat and mouse" game when determining where you should be placed within the salary range. They will have a salary in mind, but their interest is to find out what the position is worth to you. The discussion usually starts with the hiring officer asking, "What type of salary are you looking for?" This is not the time to tip your hand by providing a dollar amount. If you ask for too much, you may be knocked out of the running. By asking too little you place yourself in an awkward position, for you will undervalue the skills that you bring to the organization.

There are generally two options that you may use to answer this question. The first option places the ball in the interviewer's court and is a more direct method. We also believe that this is the most challenging of the two and is usually used when the candidate has a lot of confidence in being offered the position.

One potential response is as follows:

"Although money is important, I'm more interested in finding the right position where I am capable of using my skills. I don't have a hard number to present to you. What do you feel is a respectable salary for the position?"

A second option is less direct:

"Although money is important, the position is very impressive. I don't have sufficient information to determine a salary. I'm certain that you have a well-thought-out compensation plan that will adequately address this position."

Should the hiring officer present a salary that is below your expectation, you may choose to show some concern by pausing silently as though you are thinking over the suggested dollar amount. A second way to show your concern is to thank the hiring officer for the information and emphasize the skills you would bring to the organization that would warrant additional financial consideration. There is no need to be confrontational during this discussion, nor does it need to be prolonged at that time. Remember, wages aren't everything.

You should also explore the other benefits that are associated with the position. You may find that the total package more than exceeds your expectation. Bonus plans and the frequency of the bonus payout, health care package, the 401K program match, and other elements of the program are important considerations, as well.

Remember: Look at the Total Package You're Being Offered.

Accepting the Job Offer

Generally speaking, after the salary and benefits hurdle has been resolved, you may be offered the position, subject to passing the company physical, if required. Remember, you do not need to render a decision at that moment. Let the hiring officer know that you wish to think about the offer and discuss it with family members before committing. It is best to arrange a date and time (not to exceed 48 hours) to convey your decision.

Should you accept the offer, the company will arrange for the physical and confirm the employment opportunity. Once the final hurdle is passed, the hiring officer will generally make a telephone contact and arrange for a start date and on-boarding. This telephone contact is usually followed by a final written offer letter confirming the job and all the particulars. It is always a wise idea to follow up with a written acceptance letter. An example of such a letter follows.

Example 6-1

JERRY P. LEWIS

1212 Holly Lane * Tangle Wood, LA 45032(H) 890-855-4953 * J.Lewis@email.com

Date

Recipient Name
Title
Company
Address
City, State, Zip

Dear _____,

It is with a great deal of gratitude and enthusiasm that I accept the position offering you have extended to me. I look forward to reporting to work on the _____ day of _____ (month) to begin my on-boarding process.

Should you need to reach me in the interim please feel free to do so.

Sincerely,

Jerry P. Lewis

CONGRATULATIONS!!!

You've Landed That New Position

CHAPTER 7: THANK GOODNESS THE PROCESS IS OVER... OR IS IT?

Now that you've landed that new position it's time to begin establishing your credentials within the organization. In fact most companies have an assessment period that may last between ninety to one-hundred and twenty days where the new employee competencies are evaluated. This evaluation process holds true for both management and non-management personnel alike. The evaluation process is generally more subtle with managerial employees.

SUGGESTIONS FOR MANAGEMENT EMPLOYEES

Let's focus our attention on the first ninety days of your employment for it is one of the most critical periods for both you and the hiring organization. This stage is considered the probationary period for many reasons. First, it will allow both you and the hiring organization time to evaluate and determine that you are a suitable fit. Second, should your hiring involve a recruiting firm, there is generally a ninety day guarantee that is negotiated between the agency and hiring organization. That means that if you find yourself in an employment situation where either you or the hiring organization is dissatisfied with the employment arrangement, the placement service is usually responsible for finding another suitable candidate for the position without additional charge.

When you first come on-board and take the reins of your new position, most companies will require you to participate in some form of orientation program. Some companies have a very formal program that may last several days; others have an informal program that is conducted by a Human Resources representative and your hiring manager.

AS YOU LEARN MORE ABOUT THE ORGANIZATION, KEEP IN MIND THE FOLLOWING SUGGESTIONS:

- As you settle in, you will be introduced to everyone. You won't remember all the names at first; so that's why it's important to get an in-house phone directory as soon as possible. On your phone list jot down key words next to the names of those people you met. This will assist you in remembering faces, positions, and names.
- Observe how things get done. Who holds the clout in the organization? Who do you go see when things need to be done quickly? Who can answer questions that require answers rapidly?
- If you have a staff, have a meeting with the total team to help you get a grasp on the projects in progress. Tell your team members that you plan to meet with them one-on-one within the week. Make certain that they are prepared to provide a project update list in greater detail: their updated job description, where they feel their strengths rest, and a list of skills that they feel could be improved upon if more training is provided. This meeting will help you learn more about their jobs, current objectives, key talents, and areas for improvement. It will also set the tone for the development of mutual respect and trust.
- Set appointments to visit the colleagues you will be working with. Find out about their job responsibilities and what they feel they will need from you and your department in the future. Again, you are developing trust and cooperation.
- Observe the workplace environment and corporate culture. How are employees treated? How are work assignments given to others? How are meetings conducted?
- Meet with your boss to jointly determine your short and long term objectives. After all, this is what you will be measured against.
- After your meeting with the boss, ensure that your objectives and those of your subordinates are aligned.
- Have team meetings more frequently at first. Develop an agenda and stay on track. Demonstrate to you employees your willingness to listen and assist.
- Continue to create your action plan for the next six months and be accessible to your team members.
- Develop a style of walking around and visiting with your team members regularly.

SUGGESTIONS FOR NON-MANAGERIAL, TECHNICAL, REGULAR DAYS PAID EMPLOYEES

Should your position be a non-managerial, technical, or days paid employee, you will be expected to also participate in an orientation program. This program provides you with a great deal of helpful information. The reasoning behind the orientation is simple, it lets you know what you can expect from the company and, in return, what the company expects from you.

After the orientation you will still need to demonstrate your talents, skills, and abilities. You just do it a bit differently from your management counterpart. Remember that you will also face a probationary period. This period may be ninety days and will normally not exceed six months.

During this probationary period there are generally several performance evaluations that will be conducted where you will sit down with your boss and have an open discussion of your progress over a specific period in time. This formal evaluation lets you know how you are developing and where you currently stand. Look at it as a time for communication and learning.

AS YOU LEARN MORE ABOUT THE ORGANIZATION, KEEP IN MIND THE FOLLOWING SUGGESTIONS:

- Get to know your co-workers as soon as you can. Be outgoing and pleasant.
- When you don't understand something, don't be afraid to ask your supervisor or fellow employees for their assistance.
- Observe the workplace environment. How are employees treated? How are work assignments given to others? How are meetings conducted? Are you provided with all the information you need to complete a job assignment?
- Contribute your knowledge in team meetings. Take an active part in things that affect you.
- Be enthusiastic, alert, and eager to learn new things.
- Remember that even though you may know how to do something, some companies may require you to do the project using their method not yours. Be open to suggestions and change.

A FINAL BIT OF ENCOURAGEMENT

Whether you're a member of management or a technical employee, remember that your hiring manager is there to assist. He is a stake holder in this hiring arrangement and doesn't what you to fail. His intent is in your succeeding and can be your biggest supporter through the various stages of your employment.

Hiring Managers will tell you that at the end of the day, all they seek is an employee that:

- Meets and exceeds job performance standards
- Is seen as a team player
- Enjoys the work being done
- Contributes to the growth of the business
- Is upwardly mobile and capable of achieving even greater success
- Sees the organization as a good place to work
- Is cooperative and pleasant to work with

Here's hoping that you will reach that standard of excellence in your new organization.